Decorative Painting, Folk Art Style

PATTERNS AND EASY STEPS TO CREATING UNIQUE
FURNITURE • TOYS • GIFTS

by

Joyce Davies Hundley

Jeanne Davies Cole

DOUBLEDAY & COMPANY, INC., GARDEN CITY, NEW YORK

LIBRARY OF CONGRESS CATALOG CARD NUMBER 70–150928

If you were curious enough to open this book, we will assume that you have spare time and are looking for a way to spend it. Even with car pools for Brownies or full-time jobs, it seems that everyone nowadays is looking for a craftwork pastime, relaxing hobbies to give vent to their creative urge. Some want the quickest *fun* means to an end and bog down when a venture becomes too technical and complicated. For them and all lighthearted, imaginative souls, we present our primer on decorative painting of folk art. Here we present to you the most simple and direct ways to create a charming hand-painted piece of furniture, toy or a little gift item. We have found lots of short cuts that will make the job easier and quicker. So, if folk art is your new adventure, this book is for you.

Joyce and Jeanne

Contents

DECORATIVE PAINTING, FOLK ART STYLE

A Word on Folk Art

Folk art (or peasant art) is the handicraft of people without formal training in the arts. It is the contact between creative expression and utilitarian articles used daily by ordinary people. Although it includes such things as ceramics, glass, weaving, woodcarving and costume, we will deal here only with our dearest love, painted furniture and accessories.

The folk artists were mostly country folk who painted and whiled away long evenings after their work in the fields. While the professional artists were occupied with painting for the kings and their courts, the rural man and his neighboring craftsmen produced the more simple and unsophisticated art for each other. The craftsmen were influenced by what was being done in the courts, but were limited by their materials and training, and their work was done in a more simple manner.

The folk artist is generally anonymous, for he merely painted decorations on his furniture and household items to brighten his home and for the pure joy of painting. He had a love of color and decoration—of hearts, birds, and tulips, painted in rich blues, earthy reds and bright greens. He painted the sun, the tree of life and other symbols dating back into the past.

Folk art is a world-wide happening, centuries old, that seems to stem from the innate desire of these unsophisticated country people to beautify their homes and possessions. The most utilitarian objects were hand carved or painted, filled with expressive designs. Most of the work was done well because the people found joy in expressing themselves in a natural way.

It was in the late 1800s that collectors began to take an interest in folk art, and soon museums, too, were beginning to acquire fine examples of carved and painted pieces. As the industrial revolution was beginning to blanket the world with machine-made products, the art of the craftsman was threatened with extinction.

The demand for antique painted furniture is great and most of what is available now is priced beyond the pocketbook of the average person. You will notice that in smart shops everywhere it is the current hand-painted items that are among the most choice of the selection. Furniture manufacturers are attempting on a mass production scale to achieve the effect of hand-painted furniture. They are producing marvelous things, but their products remain mass produced and not one of a kind.

You can accomplish what they cannot. You can express your own personality and surroundings by creating your own folk art designs, something that is uniquely yours. Relax and enjoy the painting of it. Do not feel bound by rules and formulas. We will start you off in the right direction and hope that, like a baby learning to walk, you will let loose of the hand and "do your own thing."

CHAPTER ONE

Junk to Riches

CHOOSING SOMETHING TO PAINT

Many years ago, on spending some time in Provincetown, Massachusetts, we happened upon Peter Hunt's shop and there were introduced to folk art painting. In the years since and in the many phases of art that we have worked, it was always to the happy and free folk art designs that we turned for relaxation and fun. Research and study brought to us the Tyrol with its country rooms and rustic painting. One sees farmhouse-style furniture in country colors of red, blue and dark-green backgrounds with floral motifs that make furniture glow like jewels.

The designs we painted were not authentic reproductions but adaptations, a more modern version for our needs. For our small children as they were growing up, there were rooms to decorate, gifts to make, Christmas cookies to decorate. And it was the folk art motifs that people have used for centuries that were our greatest joy.

And so I was not surprised when Jeanne came by one bright autumn afternoon and said, "Let's open a shop." With that decision out of the way, there began six weeks of temporary living in the old Rambler station wagon, munching lunch during red lights and peering, poking into antique shops, secondhand stores and, yes, even junk piles.

A motley assortment of furniture began to accumulate in an appalling mass in the basement. My nephew, Jeffrey, who was four years old at the time, accompanied us on all our jaunts and to this day can't pass a wastebasket or trash pile without checking for an unexpected treasure.

Our husbands, in good-natured resignation and confident that in time this too would pass and give way to peaceful normality, polished up their tools and helped to repair, add or subtract that which was necessary. Soon the castoff furniture began to take on new character. Furniture became sound with more pleasing lines and accessories were created from odds and ends. We used color and designs to create decorative accent pieces, and you too can retrieve your discarded furniture from the attic and with some effort and fun, too, create an attractive accent piece.

Decorative painting is done in these steps:

- preparing the surface
- applying the base color
- transferring or drawing the design
- painting the design
- glazing or antiquing

The first problem—what to paint—is no problem at all! Everything but the kitchen sink! Look in the kitchen cabinets and drawers: wooden spoons or bowls, tin buckets or pails, an old table, chair, bookcase or chest of drawers. Nothing is sacred except, please and of course, your fine antiques.

Our customers have a genius for finding things for us to paint. We were once asked to paint a window in a room where there wasn't one. And a toilet seat, blue with hearts, tulips and a verse, was ordered for a Christmas gift. We painted custom-made steps for an arthritic poodle named Fifi because she could no longer jump onto the bed, and a baseball bat for a tomboy, with roses and ribbon and her name in pink. It has been said that we will paint anything you can get in the door and, really, you wouldn't believe what you *can* get through the door.

So don't overlook anything of wood or tin, large or small as a possible treasure when painted. Choose, perhaps, a child's wooden toy, a milk can, trays, a shelf, even clay flowerpots and old flatirons. Keep in mind that painted designs can lift the most humdrum item from drabness and transform it into a gay accessory.

Craft shops are springing up all over the country and offer a wide selection of unpainted items that are ready to work on. Or choose some of the well-constructed unpainted furniture that is available.

On occasion, we have painted designs on plastic which have a rather dull matte finish. The finished design on such a surface is not lasting as it would be on a wood or tin surface. After the design has been painted on plastic, with a paper towel dipped in varnish, rub the varnish sparingly over the design, much as you would apply paste wax. Care must be taken so as to not get a streaked effect.

4

Our key word is simplicity, so when choosing something to paint, look for clean simple lines. The designs you paint will provide the decoration.

FIRST AID FOR FURNITURE UGLIES

You may already have a discarded or outmoded piece of furniture that you would like to paint, or perhaps you are contemplating a furniture treasure hunt! You will find that there are many lovely things that will paint up beautifully. But please do not paint fine old antique pieces. When in doubt, a dealer can advise you which pieces should not be painted.

Be sure that the piece of furniture you choose is sound or can be repaired if necessary. If the piece is a veneered wood, check to be sure that the veneer is smooth and tight. If the veneer is loose in spots, remember that it must be glued and then held secure with clamps until the glue has dried. Oak furniture is plentiful, and when painted and glazed, the oak grain gives a beautiful textured effect to the painted finish.

While poking about in antique shops and used furniture stores, you will notice that much of the furniture is either too tall and spindly or heavily loaded with ornamental carvings. Don't overlook the possibilities of these uglies, for a little simple carpentry can work wonders in adapting this furniture to today's living. This can be one of the most rewarding and creative aspects of redoing an old piece of furniture—to change basic proportions and lines from an ugly to a lovely.

Cut down on heavy excesses of carving and trim. Much of the carving is just glued or tacked on and is easily removed with a screw driver. Be sure to sand off all traces of glue and fill with spackling paste the nail holes left by the carvings.

Tall spindly pieces possibly could benefit by sawing the legs down to a more pleasing height. Sometimes just removing the casters will improve the proportions. Old dressers, chests or radio cabinets on high legs convert to lovely low chests with legs cut to about three or four inches in height. A dining table can be made into a coffee table by shortening it to the proper height.

If you should come across an old dresser that is top heavy with the attached mirror and ornate framework, visualize the dresser alone and you will probably see a lovely simple chest, perfect for decorating. This also can apply to dressing tables which can be converted to desks and writing tables.

We suggest that you do not attempt to alter chairs. Don't saw the legs to make a lower chair, for it will never look right when cut down, not to mention how it feels to sit on such a chair. And, of course, we don't advocate surgery for that fine Chippendale highboy; good traditional styles can hardly be improved upon, so it is to the old furniture of no particular style or vintage that we direct you. Attics and secondhand stores have this sort of thing in abundance and at moderate prices for experimenting.

So, off to your treasure hunt. When you have found something that appeals to you, make any necessary repairs and then begin visualizing a new color and bright and happy designs.

Are you ready? Then let's hustle down to the paint store and gather our supplies.

SHOPPING LIST
(Ye Friendly Olde Paint Store)

Paint stores nowadays are a veritable wonderland, a potpourri of colors, potions and brews. There is a paint for everyone and for every purpose. You will find antiquing kits that will provide all the materials you will need for renovating a piece of furniture. If you are feeling lazy or just plain anxious to get to your design painting, no need to stalk to a dark corner of the store to buy an antiquing kit. Indeed, we think they are great too, so if you choose a kit, follow directions carefully and apply the design work onto the base coat and before the glazing process. Since we do a large quantity of work, antiquing kits are impractical in our studio, but we are especially fond of some of the base colors and glazes used in the Martin-Senour kits. The antique white undercoat is a good basic white and turkey red and bronze olive are two rich Early American colors that take designs beautifully.

In our studio we use either flat oil base wall paint or a satin finish enamel for the base coat, depending on the final effect desired. We suggest that you begin by using the satin enamels because the antique glaze later applied will not change the color to any great extent. At the most it will darken it slightly and give a textured effect. In using a flat paint for a base coat, the glaze will effect a considerable change. Bright red turns to a rich brownish red, bright yellow turns to mustard, and white to a deep beige. Lighter shades of blue turn toward gray and greens. These changes come about when an umber glaze is used. In Chapter Eight, glaze combinations are discussed at greater length.

For your first endeavors, we recommend a simple umber glaze as a good all-around simple approach.

Sandpaper: medium and fine

Mineral spirits: turpentine is fine but more costly and aromatic

Satin or low-gloss enamel: for your base color

Varnish: satin or flat

Antique glaze: ½ pint ready-mixed glaze in umber tone

or

½ pint can of raw-umber tinting paint (to mix
   your own glaze)

(Tube oil paint may substitute)

Brushes: 1½- and 2-inch size. Buy two, good quality (3-inch size
   for extra large surfaces)

Rubber gloves

Paper towels, cheesecloth or old rags (choose one or all)

Spackling paste

(See Chapter Three for suggested materials for the design painting)

FOR SPECIAL PROBLEMS

Bleeding stains: clear shellac and denatured alcohol (to clean
   brush) (See: *How to Prepare the Surface*)

Rust on metal: rust inhibitive paint (See: *How to Prepare the
   Surface*)

CHAPTER TWO

How to Prepare the Surface

OLD WOOD

If you have decided to transform something that is old wood, first remove all hardware such as knobs and drawer pulls and then clean the wood with soap and a damp cloth to remove all dirt and grime. Use mineral spirits, turpentine or a liquid sander to remove wax. This is very important, for paint refuses to adhere to a waxy surface and it would be most distressing to have your new paint job simply fall off in a heap on the floor.

If the piece of furniture has a very glossy varnish or painted finish, alas, much effort must be expended to sand the finish with coarse sandpaper until it is dull with "tooth" in order for it to grab a new coat of paint. If there are many, many layers of chipped paint on the surface we suggest: Move the piece back to the attic or hide it in a dark corner of the garage, or go to the aggravation of removing the old paint layers with a commercial paste-type paint remover. This is a most miserable job and worth avoiding at all costs. (See George Grotz, *Furniture Doctor;* he'll probably tell you the same thing!)

For years we have heard of clever people having heavily painted pieces "dipped" at radiator companies, and many times we have fought traffic and 95 degree temperatures carrying an especially promising piece of furniture to have dipped, only to be turned away for ridiculous reasons such as "The legs will come unglued" or "The veneer will curl." By now, you are no doubt taking that washstand back to the attic.

After you have cleaned your piece of furniture of dirt and wax, fill unsightly nail holes and cracks with spackling paste, which is quite easy to sand smooth after it has dried. When the filler has dried, sand the entire piece with medium sandpaper for good adhesion and to smooth chipped and rough areas. Some scratches and imperfections, if not disfiguring, will add a distressed and antique look to the piece after it has been given a final glaze. After you have tried a few projects you will be able to recognize just how far your sanding need go.

After sanding, remove all traces of dust with a vacuum cleaner or wipe thoroughly with a rag. You are now ready to apply the first coat of paint.

If, after applying the first coat of paint on old wood, you notice a pinkish tinge appear, the old stain in the wood is "bleeding" through. To correct this problem, wait until the base coat has dried thoroughly and then apply a coat of clear shellac over the entire piece. Allow to dry overnight and then continue with a second and final coat of your base color. Clean brushes used in shellac with a denatured alcohol.

NEW WOOD

If the piece you have chosen to paint is new wood, you can skip all the above details and just sand lightly before you apply the first coat. However, after the first coat of paint has dried you will find that the paint has raised the wood grain and given it a rough fuzzy feeling so it is necessary to give it a good sanding before you apply the second coat. It should be sanded until it is smooth to the touch.

TIN OR METAL

If your choice is an object of tin or metal, wash it well with a mixture of one-half vinegar to one-half water. This is called "etching" and is important to clean new galvanized metal such as mailboxes, pails, buckets, etc. Play it safe and etch old metals also in order to remove any greasy residue. For old metal which has rusted, remove all rust with sandpaper and then paint the piece with a rust-inhibitive paint. You can then apply your first color coat over this when it is completely dried. If the rust is not treated as we suggest it will eventually eat through the new coat of paint.

APPLYING THE BASE COLOR

The base color that you have chosen should be applied in two coats, twenty-four hours apart. Use a 2-inch brush for average size furniture, a

3-inch brush for a larger piece such as a wardrobe. Small items are easy to paint with a 1½-inch brush width. Your finished product will reflect the materials and tools with which you work, so we hope you have invested in good brushes and fresh paint.

Since folk art knows no restriction concerning color, you may like to use several contrasting or harmonizing colors on one piece. In such case, apply your base color over all surfaces for the first coat, and on the second coat, switch to the contrasting colors in the areas you choose. Imagination and originality will begin at this point.

Now that you have your piece of furniture sanded and free of all grit and dust, open your can of paint and stir it thoroughly. Be sure you have protected the floor with lots of old newspapers. Dip your brush into the paint, but not so deeply that it gets into the metal ferrule. It will be much easier to clean later and will enjoy a longer life. Each time you dip into the paint, press the brush against the rim of the can to avoid an overloaded brush, which will cause bothersome drips.

On furniture it is wise to start painting the difficult-to-reach areas first, such as desk legs, etc., finishing with the large smooth top last. Of course you have removed any drawers and taken off the drawer pulls and handles. These may be cleaned and polished with a commercial cleaner and put aside until the furniture is completely decorated. The hardware should be put back on the furniture last to give the final finishing touch.

Paint well into the wood, taking up all drips and sags with the brush. The paint may be applied in any direction, but finish the brushing with the wood grain because the direction of your brush strokes will become part of the texture pattern when the piece is antiqued or glazed.

Be sure to spend an extra few minutes to paint the sides of the drawers and the little hidden areas that will occasionally be seen. A neat base coat will pay big dividends later.

Also remember that two thin coats of paint will give you better results than one thick coat. So, give your subject a first coat, let it dry twenty-four hours, sand lightly and then give it a final coat. Occasionally, in painting on an old finish, you may find that your first coat does a good job of covering. If you find just minor irregularities in your paint job, you may be able to skip a second coat since the glaze will conceal small irregularities in the base color.

VALUABLE HINTS FOR PAINT CANS

1. Carefully make nail holes around the rim of the paint can (before you start to paint). This will allow the paint that ordinarily accumulates to drip back down into the can.

2. Before putting the can of paint aside after painting, lay a cloth over the top and seal the lid with light taps of the hammer. This will give you a tight seal without splashing paint about.

3. Your brush may sit overnight between coats in a jar of mineral spirits or turpentine to keep it from drying out. Before painting again, squeeze excess liquid from the brush with an old terry towel.

CHAPTER THREE

Selecting Supplies and Designs

"WHAT KIND OF PAINT DO YOU USE?"

Two busloads of tourists stopped by our shop one morning and eighty ladies crowded into the display rooms. It can be safely said that not one of them asked, "What kind of paint do you use?" This was understandable for they had but thirty minutes to browse in the shops along the way, so instead of chatting for a while, they went busily about their shopping.

However, many times a day we hear that question, which is one of the reasons that this book was written in the first place. For years we have been using artists' oil paints for folk art design work. The oil paints are thinned with a painting medium of one-half turpentine and one-half varnish. Since oils are slow drying and patience being our lesser virtue, there was much aggravation in painting the more elaborate designs. This was offset, however, by the wonderful possibilities of blending colors, soft transitions and a lovely transparency that only oils can give. One important rule we learned in using oils is always allow the finished design to dry good and hard before glazing over it. A protective coat of varnish before glazing is always a good precaution in protecting the design.

All of this is being mentioned so that you can see why suddenly we took a new direction. Anyone in his right mind who has ever been confronted by a shop full of frantic Christmas shoppers would immediately rack his brain for time-saving methods. And, dear reader, we found it in a product that was new to the art world at that time. Artists' acrylic paints, with all of their fast-drying qualities, were the answer to our problems. Their ease in handling, using water as a thinning medium, and their durable lasting qualities were a pure delight.

In our studio we use Liquitex acrylic artists' colors made by Permanent Pigments, Inc. In our section on color mixing we use Liquitex, and since colors do vary some according to manufacturers, color results may differ slightly with other brands.

There have been occasions when we have found it necessary to use cans of enamels for designs; however, they tend to get drippy on vertical surfaces. We once painted a washstand with floor enamel for the simple reason that it needed to be painted and that was the only available material at hand. However, we do not recommend such unconventional practices, to ensure durability at any rate.

SHOPPING LIST FOR DESIGN PAINTING

Congratulations! If you are still with us, you have survived the dirty work and now have your prize painted in a lovely shade, looking fresh and tidy, just waiting for designs to transform it into something special and uniquely yours.

An art supply store has all the materials you will need for design painting. Following is a list of materials used in our studio.

1. Tubes of artists' acrylic paints:
   > Titanium white
   > Ivory black
   > Cadmium yellow, medium
   > Yellow oxide (ocher)
   > Cadmium red, medium
   > Ultramarine blue
   > Oxide of chrome (chrome green)
   > Raw umber
   > Red oxide or burnt sienna

2. Red sable watercolor brushes: Sizes 2, 5, 8, 10
   (Buy as fine a quality as you can afford; poor brushes can be a severe handicap!)
3. Disposable palette (or a plate is a good substitute)
4. Graphite paper (for transferring designs)
5. Tracing paper
6. Paper towels

CHOOSE YOUR DESIGN

And now, down to this thing called folk art! In choosing your design, keep in mind that there are actually no rules in folk art. We are merely presenting to you this guide on what has been done before, so relax and enjoy yourself.

Look carefully at your subject. Large pieces of furniture seem to look better with large designs, small pieces with smaller designs. The proportion of a design will pretty much determine the area where it will be placed. That is, a vertical design will fit on a vertical panel, while a horizontal design is ideal for a drawer. Spaces look best when filled adequately with design and not broken up by many small clusters.

Folk art in its true sense is unsophisticated, so we will consider now the more simple pieces of furniture that lean toward the primitive. In the latter part of the book there are the more sophisticated urban type of French and Italian designs for the furniture with more elegant lines.

Consider the use of the piece of furniture that you have chosen to decorate. Will you want it decorated in the spirit of the room where it will be used? Imagine fruits and vegetables for the kitchen, nursery stories for a child's room. Grape clusters and wine glasses would be appropriate for a wine cabinet. A lovely floral design is fine most anywhere in the house.

Some of the designs we offer you are variations of the Pennsylvania Dutch, which are very similar to much of the painted European peasant furniture and accessories. The same familiar motifs appear again and again: the heart, tulip, birds, flowers and stars. These symbols were often primitively conceived but when painted in bright colors, they provided some of the few ornamentations the country folk had.

You will find that the designs in this book can be used in a number of ways and will seem different on contrasting pieces of furniture or in different color combinations.

Don't worry about whether the design is perfectly centered or that the heart is lopsided. Don't fret for hours about this color going with that color. The folk artist had an inherent love of color and showed no restraint in its use. So be not of timid heart; use color in your designs, pure and rich, and really enjoy painting them.

You will find yourself quite attached to your work of art by the time you have finished, so make it a part of your home. Use it to brighten a dull corner. Don't be afraid to use it! The very old painted peasant furniture that is seen in museums today shows many years of wear, with scars and worn-off paint. This acquired patina of time is truly a thing of beauty.

HOW TO TRANSFER A DESIGN

It would be better if you could sketch your design directly onto the surface to be painted. This should be done lightly in pencil. The pencil marks that still show after the design is dry can be erased.

If you are one who has proudly announced that you can't draw a straight line (straight lines can be more difficult than curved ones, especially if you are nervous), then we will assume that you mean you cannot draw at all. Have no fear! You CAN paint if you will trace our designs and use our methods!

With a piece of tracing paper and pencil, trace the design that you wish to use directly from the book. Transfer this pattern to your painting surface by placing a piece of graphite paper (graphite side down) over the place to be decorated. Place the tracing paper pattern over the graphite and secure with Scotch tape. Trace over the outlines of the design with a sharp pencil or ball-point pen. We recommend that you not substitute carbon paper for the graphite because it will leave a greasy residue that will keep the paint from adhering to your surface. Be sure to go over all of the lines. Too mechanical? Not very artistic? Not so, for you will find that tracing over the design will familiarize you with the rhythm of it and thus prepare you for painting.

If the background of your painting surface is dark and the pencil tracings do not show, rub white chalk on the back of your tracing as a substitute for the graphite paper.

ENLARGING A DESIGN

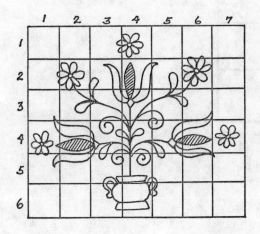

If you have an especially large surface that calls for a larger design than you find in the book, it is possible to enlarge any of the designs by the following method:

Trace the design from the book onto a piece of tracing paper. With a ruler, measure and mark off equal squares directly on your tracing.

15

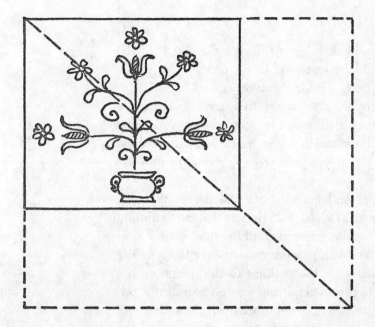

Place another piece of tracing paper over your design and draw in the top and left-side lines of the rectangle, extending them beyond the original ones.

Now draw a diagonal line, extending it beyond the original design until you reach the size that you want for the enlargement. Complete the larger rectangle.

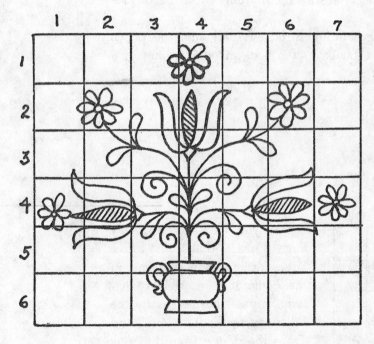

Mark off this rectangle with exactly the same number of squares. Number each square both up and down so that they correspond exactly with the original design.

Copy each line from every square into the corresponding square, doing one square at a time.

CHAPTER FOUR

Painting with Acrylics

Acrylic paints are made with a plastic base and are thinned to a painting consistency with water. When the water evaporates, a strong binder remains, which is highly adhesive and waterproof. The colors are brilliant and durable. The acrylic paints dry rapidly so there is no delay in completing a painted design. Because of these fast-drying properties, care must be taken to keep the brushes wet while you are working with acrylics. Don't allow the paint to dry in the brush. Rinse the brush with water to clean it when changing colors. When you have finished painting, wash the brush with bar soap and water before putting it aside.

You may use a glass or porcelain plate as a palette, for the paint is easily removed from these surfaces when water is applied.

Acrylic colors dry with a low sheen, almost a matte finish, and can be varnished.

COLOR MIXING

Looking at the list on page 13, you will notice that we have restricted the palette to seven colors plus black and white. Too many colors in a design can create a confused appearance. With these colors you can mix an adequate variety of colors. Theoretically, any color can be mixed by using the primary colors, red, yellow and blue. Surely everyone knows that yellow and blue make green and that red and yellow make orange. Many people don't know but quickly discover that when you mix too many colors you get *mud*. So you see, there are a few things that we would like to tell you about color mixing that will get you started on the right track and then you can go about making happy discoveries of your own.

If you should develop a real yen for flower painting, you will quickly find that there are certain colors that will be impossible to mix with the basic palette, which we have recommended to you. These will be the violets, blue pinks and purples. Acra violet and dioxazine purple in the tubes may be added to your palette for a wider range of floral colors.

The less mixing you do, the cleaner and fresher your color will be. Beware of using too much white in mixing colors for you will get an undesirable chalky effect. In much of the folk painting the colors are used pure and rich.

With a medium-size brush, try mixing some of the following combinations:

REDS:

- Various shades of pink and rose can be obtained by changing the proportions of cadmium red and white. For a light pink, gradually add red to white until the desired depth of pink is reached. For dark pink and rose tones, begin with red and add white gradually.
- By adding yellow oxide to red you will get an orange red, and added to pinks will give a range of peach colors.
- Flesh or skin tones are made by adding a little yellow oxide to a very pale pink.
- A slight addition of blue to all shades of pink will give a more neutral dusty pink.
- An addition of black or raw umber to red will give a range of deep reds.

BLUE:

- A range of blues beginning with the palest blue and working back to the pure ultramarine blue is obtained merely by the amount of white added.
- For a darker blue, add black gradually, working toward the shade desired.
- Adding raw umber to the blue will give it a more neutral tone.
- Try adding one of the yellows to blue for a different variety of green.

YELLOW:

- White added to cadmium yellow produces a lemon color.
- White added to yellow oxide will produce a cream color.

18

- Yellow oxide, white and raw umber will give a tan or beige color.
- Reds and yellows create oranges.
- Yellow oxide is a rich golden color that frequently we use directly as it comes from the tube.
- Cadmium yellow and raw umber produce a mustard color.

GREEN:

- Chrome green is a warm hue that is very useful in itself but has limited mixing qualities. By adding yellow oxide you can obtain an avocado green and by adding cadmium yellow, a spring green. Touches of white can be added for variation.
- Small amounts of raw umber added to green and yellow give a neutralized leaf green for floral designs.
- Add blue to green for turquoise and then a touch of white for aqua.
- Add black for a darker green.
- Greens can be toned down toward olive by adding red.

BLACK:

- Black and yellow make an interesting green.
- Outlining a design in black will give emphasis to your design and brighten the colors.
- Black and white make a cold gray. A touch of yellow oxide to black and white will make a warm gray. Or try a touch of red or blue for interesting grays.

RED OXIDE or BURNT SIENNA:

- This is a good rust color straight from the tube. Add black for brown or dark brown.

CHAPTER FIVE

Painting the Design, Step by Step

Gather your tubes of paint, palette and a jar of water for cleaning your brush when you thin the paint or change colors. Use a paper towel for removing excess water from your brush.

Squeeze an adequate amount of paint in the colors you will be using onto your palette. Begin with a blob of each color about the size of a dime, no less, for it will cause you to be stingy with your paint and will make the design appear weak and miserly. If you squeeze more than that at a time, the paint will form a skin and dry out. If you find the paint on the palette is drying too rapidly, a fine spray of water from an old Windex bottle will keep the paint moist.

Mix colors with the tip of the brush, never allowing paint to seep into the metal ferrule of the brush. When finished painting for the day, always wash the brush with soap and water.

Your work will usually begin with the largest brush and work down to the smaller ones for finishing details. When in doubt, use a larger brush rather than a smaller one. This will prevent you from making tight-looking strokes. Remember, this is a fun experience and if you are uptight, best go jog around the shopping center until you can relax.

Begin by establishing the large basic color areas; details can be added later. Paint areas of one color one at a time. Lay your colors in flat and smooth. Try to avoid too much blending with acrylics. Simplify! This will give your work a decorative quality that carries well and is quite striking. If you must shade, think in terms of simple areas, the lights and darks.

Paint medium tones first, then lights, putting darks in last. Keep the source of light consistent. Think shadow side and light side in order to avoid confusion.

Practice on a sheet of paper for rich, fluent and abundant strokes. Too much water to thin the paint to a flowing consistency will cause a thin look in your design. Too much mixing of paints will create a muddy overpainted look.

Great results are attained by the pressure, force or delicacy with which your stroke is made. It is possible to get a great variety of effects by handling your brush with freedom and ease. Whenever possible, begin the stroke at the wide end and taper it by lifting the pressure on the brush.

All right, let's practice! On a piece of paper we will now learn to do the key stroke. It has been called the basic stroke, the eyebrow stroke, feather stroke, and can be seen in folk painting dating centuries back. Add a little water to a blob of paint on your palette until it is the consistency of thick cream. Using your large brush that tapers to a fine point, stroke the brush into the paint until it is nicely loaded. Hold the brush almost at a right angle to the paper and steady your hand with your little finger.

Press down on the brush and begin to draw it toward you, gradually letting up on the pressure until just the tip touches the paper. Make straight exclamation marks and curled comma-like strokes. Practice, practice, practice! Master your brush, master your strokes, and you will be able to paint your design. Make a heart with two comma strokes, then fill it in at the center. For illustration of this basic brush stroke see photographs 12–16.

Try painting a tulip with just three strokes

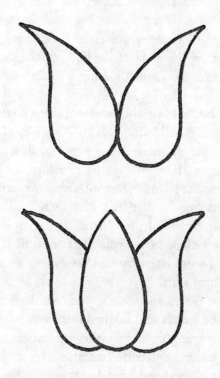

. . . and practice some more!

Let's try a variation of the comma and exclamation stroke. You have discovered by now that the amount of pressure applied to the brush is the secret to varying the strokes. So let's try a ribbon stroke. Apply pressure and then let up and then apply pressure without lifting your brush from the paper. Reload your brush at a light pressure point and continue.

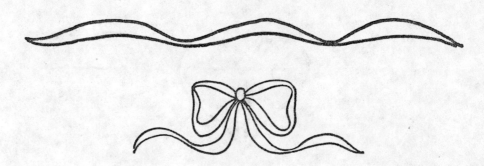

Now paint a daisy.

A leaf. Begin with light pressure, bear down and then let up.

Everyone should know how to paint a house. So begin by blocking in a flat color. Apply your paint smoothly and evenly and if it does not cover well the first time, wait a few minutes to let it dry and give it a second coat. Do not attempt to use your paint too thickly, but try to keep it at a smooth flowing creamlike consistency.

Flat color . . .   add comma strokes . . .   then final line detail

Now you may begin to combine these basic exercises and zounds zooks, you have yourself a design!

HEART: Mix cadmium red and white. Paint a pink heart!

Add a pure red heart inside, then green leaves.

TULIP: Mix blue and white. Paint a light blue tulip.
Add deep blue accents, green stem and leaves.

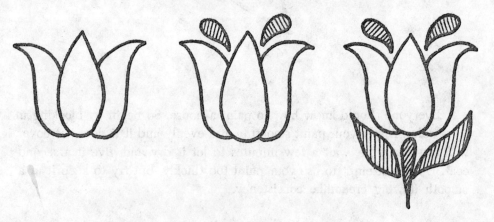

Now altogether! A complete design for a drawer front or chair back.

Or add another heart to enlarge your design to fit a headboard of a bed.

ROSE: Paint a pink circle. Add red petals, green stem and leaves.

Combine roses with hearts and tulips.

ANGEL: It's easy when you paint simple areas first!
Paint the face in flesh tones.

Next, the wings in yellow oxide.

Brown hair and brown collar.

Red edges on the wings and rosy cheeks.

Outline if you like or you might just paint the details (face, feathers, halo) in either black or raw umber!

Paint large areas first, and one color at a time. *Simple!*

CHAPTER SIX

Easy to Paint Designs

PEASANT DESIGNS

You can see that it is possible to take separate elements and combine them in a variety of ways to create your own original designs. This is especially effective with the peasant designs and even though you may be inexperienced in drawing and painting we would like to suggest that you at least try your hand at this. On the next few pages you will find many single design elements that should stir your imagination. Pick and choose those you like best and combine them to tell a story. Let your imagination work for you and if your interpretation is different from anything in this book, all the better: it will reflect *your* personality, your likes and dislikes. Paint little figures of people to represent those you know. Paint pets, your house, trees, lakes and roads. If there is something you would like to say, paint it in your own handwriting. Put names on it to identify its owner. Paint in simple cheery colors and make it happy and interesting.

Angels are favorites with us and we paint them on just about anything; angels with painted rosy cheeks, corkscrew curls or hair flying as they soar through clouds. They are sophisticated angels or they have Buster Brown haircuts and freckles with huge B-29 wingspreads or tiny wings that would not lift them from the ground.

Paint those subjects that you love and you will find it is not difficult to do. Jump right in and get your feet wet.

Little girls love angels on boxes, sconces, toy chests.

Paint a village, put people in it.

Tell a story.

Have your people doing things.

Borders

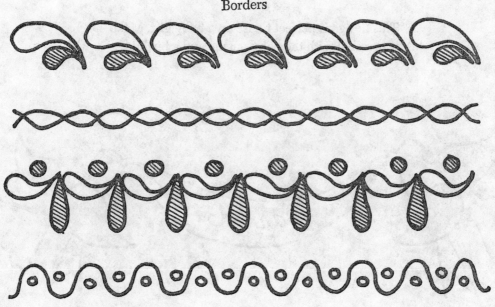

This design is perfect to use on a baby gift. Make
it personal with the baby's name and a birthday.

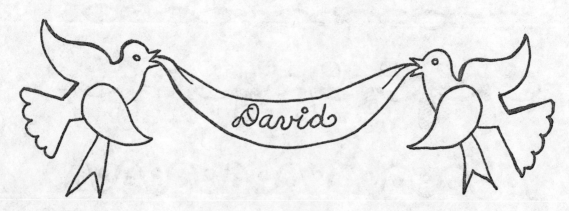

Welcome!

PENNSYLVANIA DUTCH DESIGNS

From the seventeenth through the nineteenth centuries, the decorative painting of America flourished in New England and Pennsylvania. By the year 1776, nearly half of the residents of Pennsylvania had migrated from the area of the upper Rhine in Europe. The descendants of these German and Swiss people became known as the Pennsylvania Dutch. Most of their painted decorations were derived from the old world, a happy blend of the delicate Swiss designs with the bold bright designs of the Germans. Among the migrants came farmers, potters and printers. They brought their love of color and decoration and painted the same familiar designs on their barns, furniture and household utensils.

The early furniture was painted by the man who built it, but later the painting was given out to shops and itinerant artists who traveled from farm to farm spreading local news and sometimes working for only their room and board. They did any decorating job that was needed; hex signs on the barn for good luck and decoration, bridal chests and other pieces of furniture, and even interior decorating. Red was one of the favorite colors. Pastels were usually considered washed-out looking.

The Pennsylvania Dutch folk artist painted in simple bright colors. In painting your designs use lots of yellows, reds and browns, often pure and in flat tones. Paint simply and fill the areas well. Many of the designs may be outlined in black. Try writing names, dates and expressions in some of your designs.

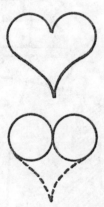

HEART: The heart was generally painted fatter than in other folk art, perhaps because it was often drawn with a compass.

It signifies love of God or love and romance.

TULIP: The three petals represent the Trinity. Many interpretations of the tulip can be found in Pennsylvania Dutch art.

DISTLEFINK:
The good luck bird

PEACOCK

POMEGRANATE

OTHER SYMBOLS:

Unicorn (virginity) Hex signs
Mermaids Scrolls and lettering
Double-headed eagle Angels (most often placed
Fruits and flowers at the top—near heaven)

Flowers

Unicorn

Angel

Distlefink

37

PENNYSLVANIA DUTCH EXPRESSIONS:
    It wonders me! (Amazes)
    Make the door shut. (Close the door.)
    Outen the light. (Turn off the light.)
    The bell don't make. (Ring)
    Kissin' don't last, cookin' do.

These are fun to use with your designs.

The Pennsylvania Dutch fractur paintings are a fine source for design ideas. Fractur is the term used in referring to ink drawings combined with watercolor. (The word fractur is actually the name of a sixteenth-century German type face.) Pennsylvania Dutch fractur derived from European manuscript illumination, elaborate hand lettering, which was used before the invention of printing by machine.

The art was brought to America where it was simplified: Lettering became subordinate to the elaborate designs. As the painting became more important, fractur developed into a folk art in the form of certificates and documents—wedding and birth certificates provide many delightful designs.

1. Here's a set of before-and-afters: a wash-stand with a clumsy mirror and frame (and no obvious antique beauty) can become . . .

2. . . . this piece, with a warm Early American mustard color base coat, green trim, strawberry designs (see page 65). The mirror has been detached and coordinates.

3. A furniture ugly, a console from an old dining room set: It is a good example of excessive ornamental trim.

4. After, with legs cut down, gingerbread trim removed, it is painted avocado with ivory panels. The design on page 46 transforms it to a Pennsylvania Dutch blanket chest.

STEP BY STEP

5. Fill holes and unsightly cracks with spackling paste.

8. Apply glaze with a brush or rag. Be sure to get into all cracks or crevices, and apply generously.

9. Remove excess glaze by rubbing with the grain of the wood, leaving darker tones in the cracks and corners. The center is usually rubbed lighter.

6. The base coat is painted well into the wood, taking up all drips and sags. Finish with strokes in the direction of the wood grain.

7. Paint the design by establishing the large color areas first, add detail last.

10. Use a soft dry brush to blend the light and dark areas.

11. Pull spatula or stick over the bristles for a fine spray of spatter.

BASIC BRUSH STROKE

12. Begin stroke by pressing down on the brush and drawing it toward you.

13. Gradually let up on the pressure until just the tip of the brush touches.

PAINT A ROSE

14. Paint a pink circle.

15. Add two red petals on each side.

16. Then a green stem and leaves.

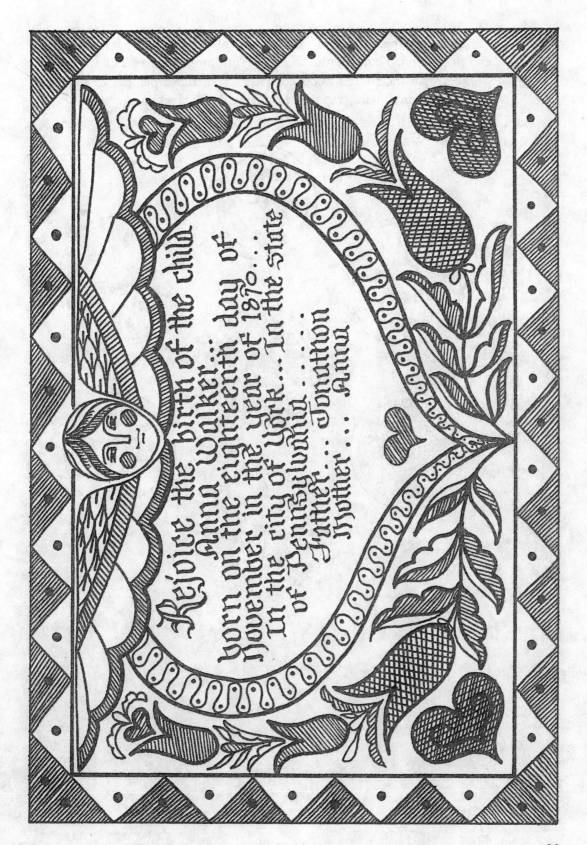

Rejoice the birth of the child Anna Walker... born on the eighteenth day of November in the year of 1870... In the city of York... In the State of Pennsylvania... Father... Jonathon Mother... Anna

39

Hex signs were painted on Pennsylvania Dutch barns for good luck and decoration. They are also found on furniture and accessories. Country painters with their huge wood compasses sometimes painted as many as seven signs on a barn, ranging from four to six feet in diameter.

Double-pointed star.

One of the earliest hex signs, a six-lobed rosette.

Trace this design and then flip the pattern over and trace the other half of the hex sign. Be sure to match the center line when you turn the pattern.

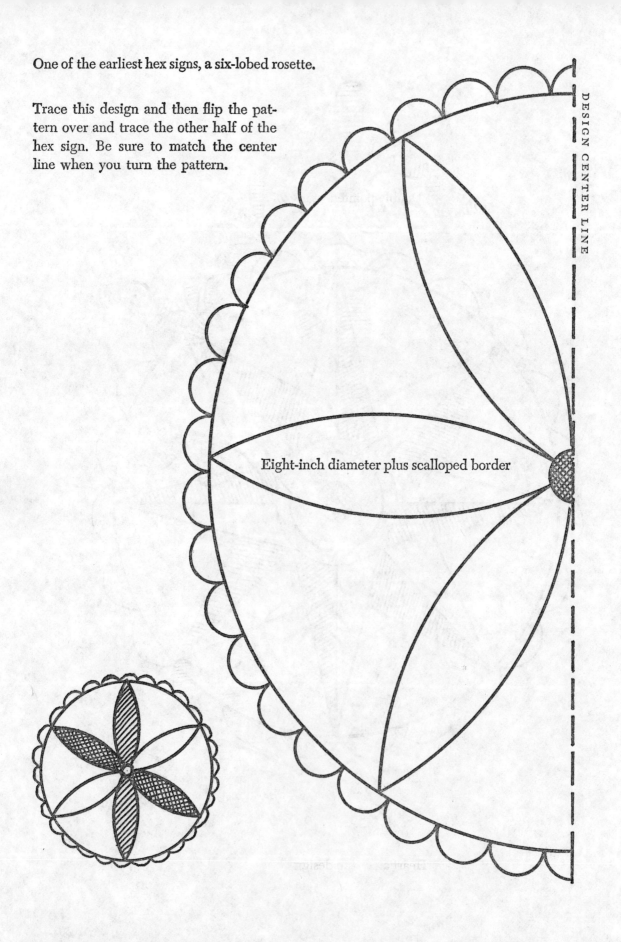

DESIGN CENTER LINE

Eight-inch diameter plus scalloped border

Heart and tulip design

Distlefink

Try these smaller designs for a box top or small accessories.

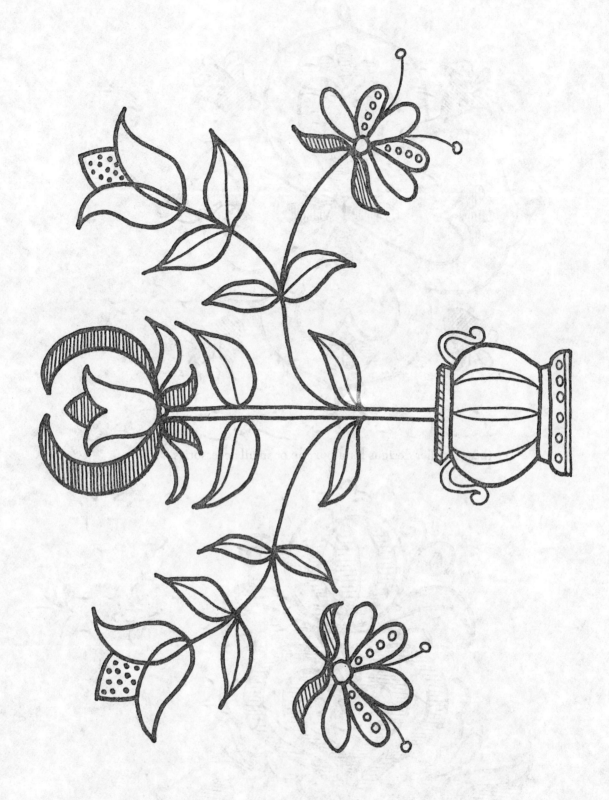

46

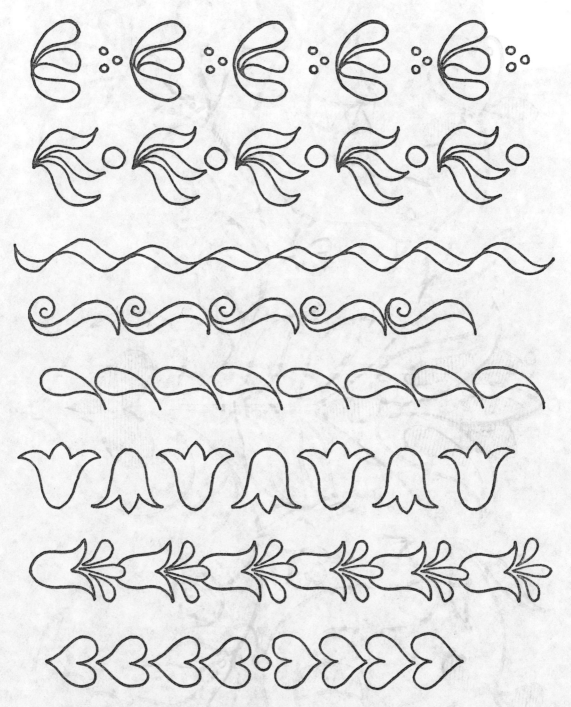

Borders can be painted in just one color or contrasting colors. Use them for framing a design or to fill blank spaces.

This design was derived from an antique bride's box.

CENTER LINE

* To repeat design on left side, reverse pattern.

Pomegranate design

TOLEWARE

The French word *tôle* actually refers to painted iron, but is used widely in reference to painted tinware. Early American tôle was done by a process called japanning. A glossy tar-base varnish was applied to the tin and then was kiln dried. It was used to imitate the Japanese lacquer finish. The freehand decoration was done in oil paints and was referred to as flowering.

Favorite toleware pieces were the crooked spout coffeepots, deed boxes, candleholders, mugs, trays and tea caddies. Many hobby shops today carry reproductions that you can paint, or perhaps at the local hardware shop you may run across tin cups, watering cans or pails that can be decorated in this manner. The most popular base colors used by the early craftsmen were: red (orange red or brownish red), black (charcoal), yellow (mustard), white (used for brides), green (rarely used).

Coffeepot

Tea caddy

Candlestick

Deed box

Cream jug

Designs typical of toleware flowering

Border

Practice for brush-stroke painting.

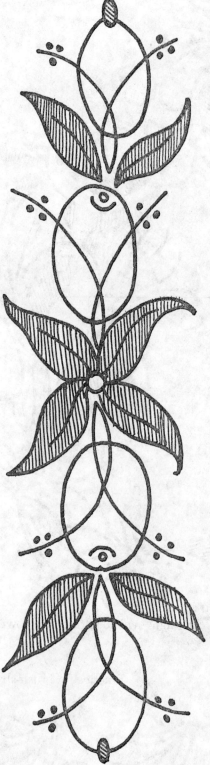

Toleware

Border. To paint gold borders use yellow
oxide or cadmium yellow and umber.

56

Toleware   Pomegranate design

57

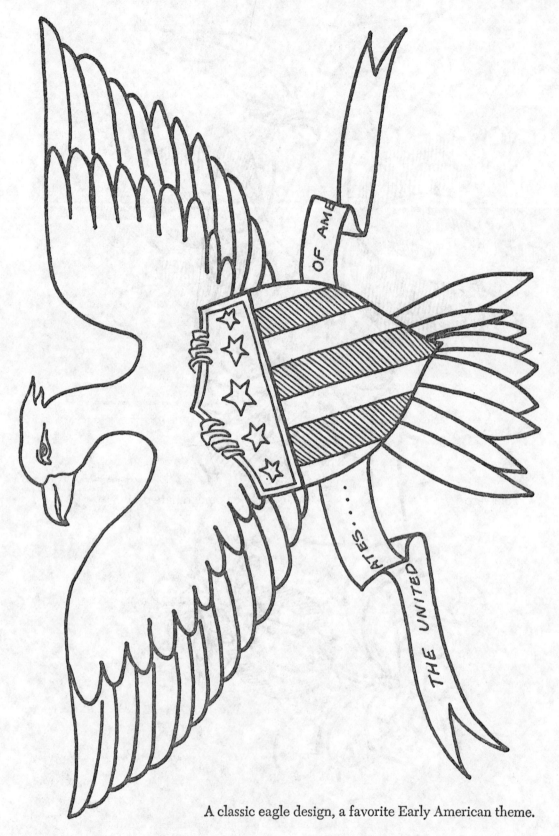

A classic eagle design, a favorite Early American theme.

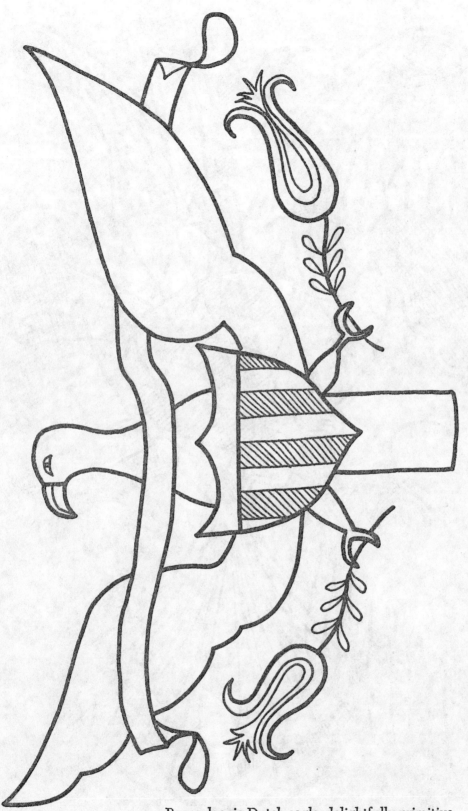

Pennsylvania Dutch eagle, delightfully primitive.

The double-headed eagle, centuries old and
a favorite with the Pennsylvania Dutch.

Romanesque eagle. An ancient design, with a modern feeling.

PAINTING FLOWERS, FRUITS AND VEGETABLES

When painting flowers, fruits and vegetables, remember that you are painting an impression, not a photographic copy. This can be done in several techniques. The brush stroke method is very effective in obtaining a stylized effect for decorating furniture and accessories. To do this, paint in the basic shape of the object in a medium tone of the color you will be using. The shadow side is put in with comma brush strokes in a deeper tone, following the contour of the subject. This will give form in a simple stylized manner. When painting flower petals, it is best to try to form a petal with one stroke only. Do not keep going over it. This is also true of leaves.

Basic shape   Add brush strokes for form.

The next method is to paint in the basic shape in a medium tone. When this is dry, paint in a shadow side in a deeper tone. Do not blend the shadows into the lighter area. Simply put in details and you will have a good contrasting effect which carries well.

The third method which is available to you is the blending method which will give a more realistic effect to flowers, fruits and vegetables. This is accomplished quite easily with artists' oil paints which are slow drying. Acrylics can be a bit more tricky. Simple blending can be accomplished in the following manner: Lay in your flat middle tone color; allow this to dry and then paint the dark tone over on the shadow side.

When this is dry, using a damp clean brush, softly brush along the edges where the two tones meet. Stop immediately when blended, for too much stroking will lift the color. Lights may be applied next and details added last. Paint leaves in light and dark tones, putting in veins last. Do not pile the paint on too thickly.

Keep in mind at all times that you are striving for an impression of the subject, not a photographic copy.

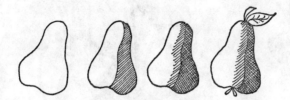

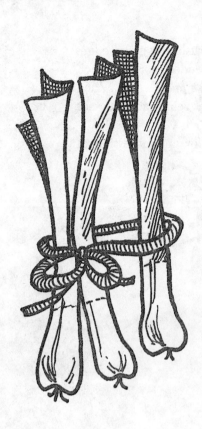

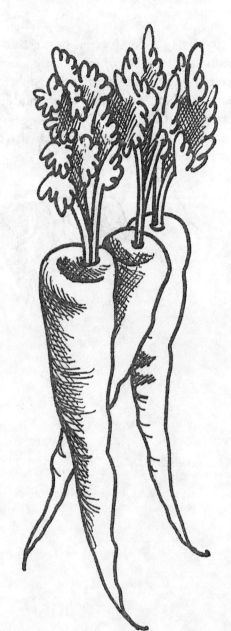

Try vegetables for the kitchen

Paint them on cabinet
doors, drawers, etc.

Idea: Use coffee cans to
make a set of cannisters.

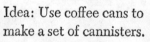

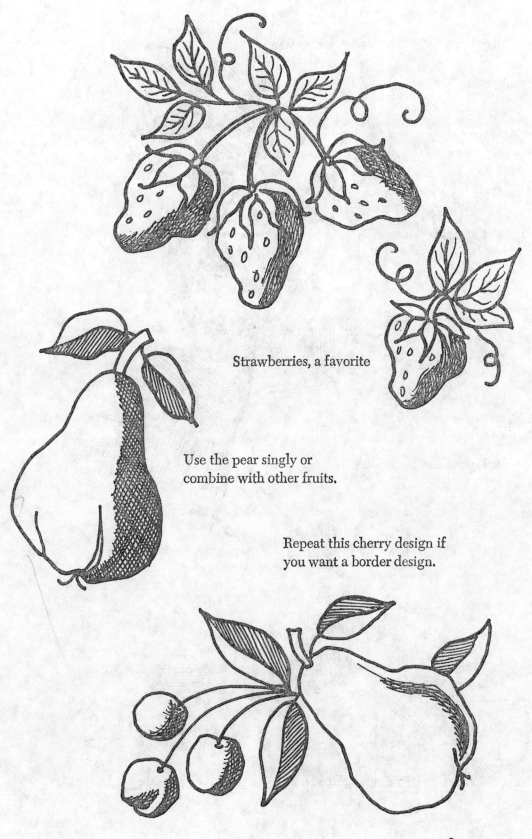

Strawberries, a favorite

Use the pear singly or
combine with other fruits.

Repeat this cherry design if
you want a border design.

Fruit and grape leaf

Paint chest all one color, or paint each drawer a different harmonizing color.

Fruit and grape leaf design is Early American and suitable for slats on a ladder-back chair.

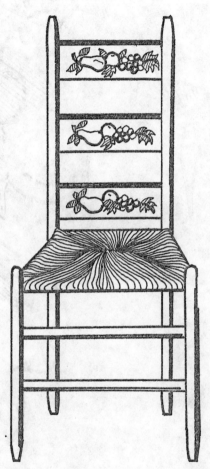

Enclose the designs with one of the borders on page 101, or design a new one of your own.

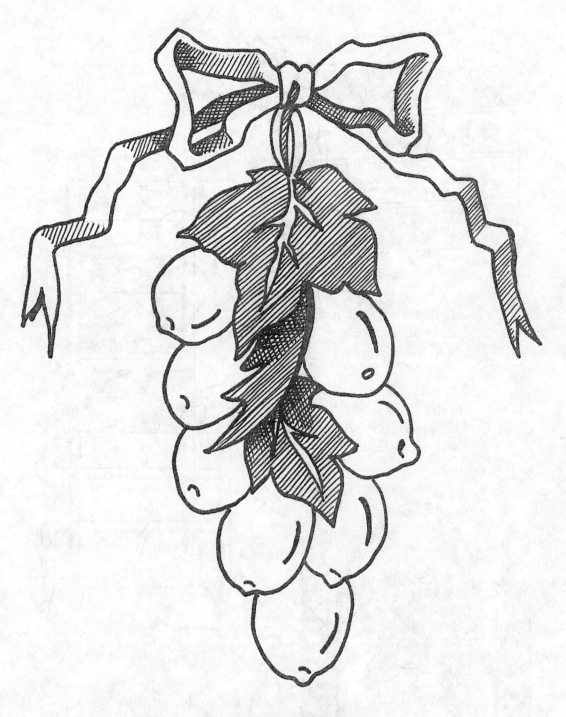

Lemon swag, rather sophisticated.
Would be stunning on a board as a wall hanging.

Ivy can be used as a design in itself or as a border.

Roses

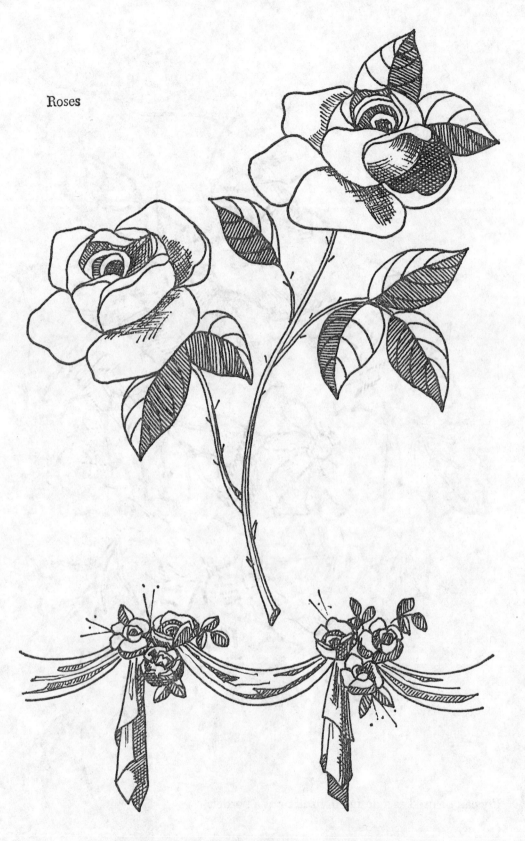

Combine roses with ribbon or swags for a continuous pattern.

Tray design.

Paint a panel.

Paint a panel if the piece lacks architectural interest.

Make an ordinary box more elegant with a panel of flowers and borders.

CHAPTER SEVEN

Contemporary Designs for Small Fry

Nurseries and children's rooms are probably the most fun of all to decorate because you have such appreciative critics. Children love bright colors and designs. Any design may be painted in any color combination such as blue horses and pink teddy bears. Red, white and blue are always popular for the boys and either bright cheerful colors or soft pastels are used in the nursery.

Do not restrict yourself to the designs included in this book. You will find children's designs in coloring books, nursery stories, Mother Goose, or in wallpaper or fabric that you have chosen to use in the room. Repeat a figure from your fabric on a cornice board, window shade or a piece of furniture.

Although the children's designs are in a contemporary vein and not folk art as such, we feel that they are an important part of decorative painting.

For a nursery

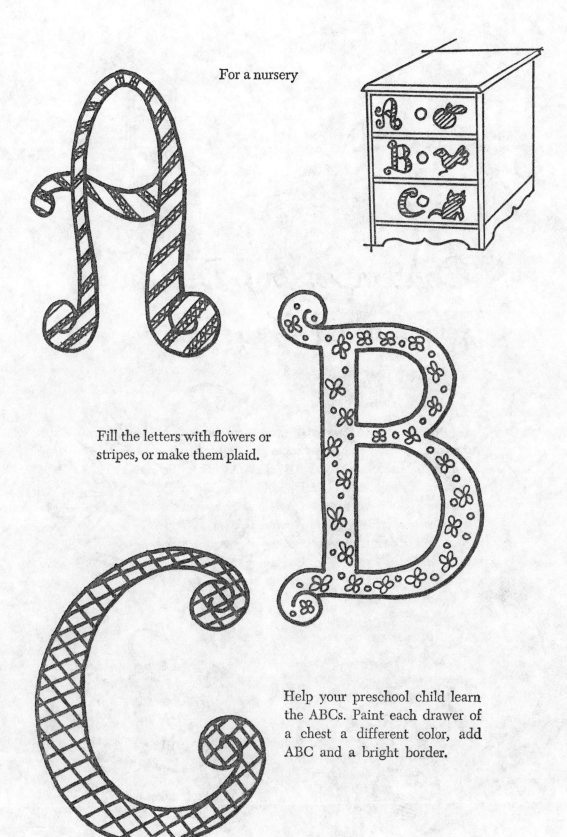

Fill the letters with flowers or
stripes, or make them plaid.

Help your preschool child learn
the ABCs. Paint each drawer of
a chest a different color, add
ABC and a bright border.

A bucket makes a fine wastebasket.

Paint a butterfly,

try adding a ribbon and daisies.

Rag dolls for toy chests, chairs, stools and boxes, or cut them out of plywood (enlarge the design for the wall).

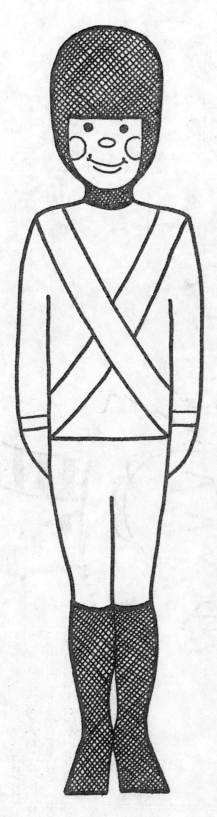

Red, white and blue

Paint a saltine cracker box white. Use this toy soldier design, add a bright border and a child's name on the top. Use it as a crayon box.

Paint a milk can to look like a drum, or use the design with the toy soldier for a military theme in a boy's room.

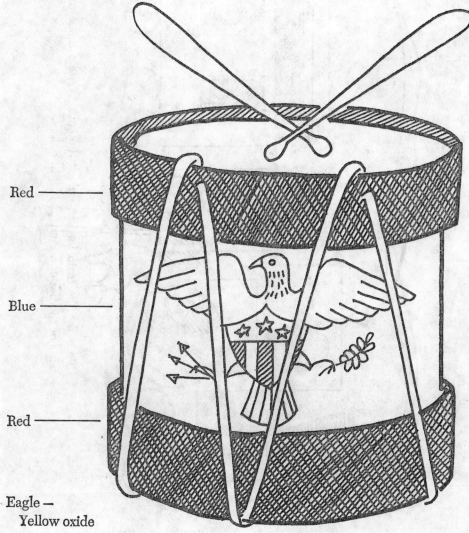

Red ————

Blue ————

Red ————

Eagle —
Yellow oxide

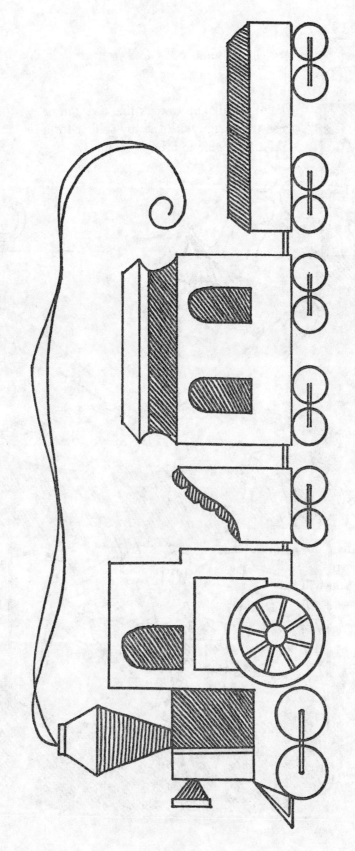

To make the train longer, repeat the cars. Write a name in smoke or on the side of the flat car. Paint in bright colors.

A little searching may turn up some odds and ends in boards. Paint a whimsical turtle or snail.

Attach at the top a brass or wooden drapery ring for a hanger, and you will have a wall plaque or two.

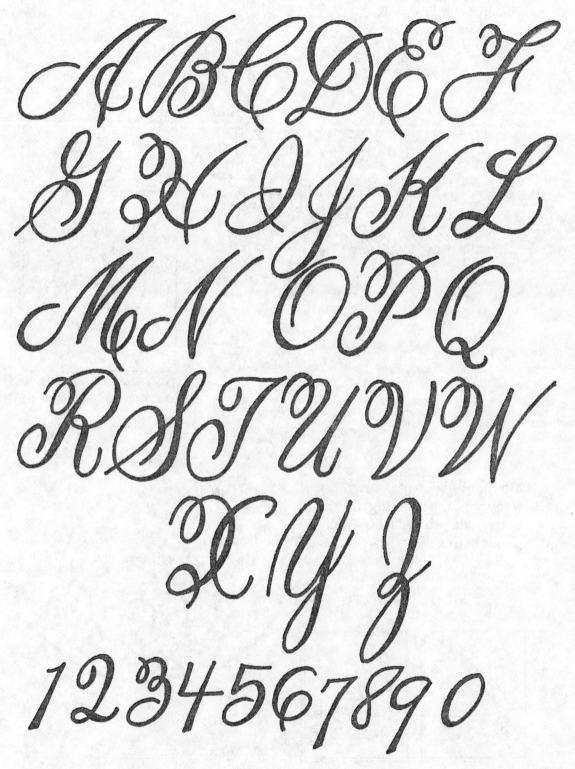

CHAPTER EIGHT

Glazing or Antiquing

Glazing will pull the entire color scheme of your painted piece into a beautifully warm, harmonious whole. This is done with a pigment and varnish solution. There are many ready-mixed solutions available that will do a fine job for you. If you prefer to mix your own, our recipe follows:

BASIC GLAZE

2 teaspoons tube oil paint or liquid tinting paint

½ cup varnish

¼ cup turpentine

A few drops of boiled linseed oil (You don't
    have to boil it, buy it that way)

Measure the oil paint into a jar and add the turpentine, mixing well. Then add the varnish and mix again. The few drops of linseed oil will keep the glaze from drying too quickly during the application.

Raw umber makes a good all-around glaze for most pieces that you choose to antique because of its transparency and rich warm character. With a few other colors added to the basic umber glaze you will have some variations from which to choose. Use artists' oil colors in tubes for this. A prepared umber glaze may also be varied in the same manner. Try the following glazes over a white base coat for a variety of effects.

GLAZE	RESULT
Raw umber and ultramarine blue	Silvery gray
Raw umber and chrome green	Delicate green cast

GLAZE	RESULT
Raw umber and burnt sienna	Reddish brown cast
Raw umber and black	Warm gray
Raw umber and raw sienna	Honey color

When mixing the above glazes, mix the basic recipe using raw umber as the tinting color. Carefully and slowly add the other required color. Test your color glaze after each addition, gradually working toward the desired color effect.

The umber glaze is satisfactory over most base colors. However, when glazing over light shades of blue, umber will turn the blue toward a greenish tinge. If you wish to retain a true blue, add either black or ultramarine blue pigment to the umber glaze.

Glazing will deepen the colors of your base coat and designs, making them richer in appearance. If you want a very light antiqued effect, the basic glaze can be "watered down" by adding more varnish. If you wish a heavier antiqued effect, use less varnish than the basic recipe requires.

When decorating furniture to be used in a contemporary setting or for brightly colored children's things, try using a deep tone of the base color in your glaze. For example, use a red glaze over pink, a deep blue glaze over pale blue, or a deep yellow glaze over lemon yellow. Try orange over yellow. Deep-colored satin enamels may be used in place of tube oil colors to tint the basic glaze. Experiment!

To "frost" a piece of furniture and attain a delicate pastel look, use white as a tinting color in the basic recipe. For a heavy frosted effect you may add four more teaspoons of white paint than the recipe normally calls for.

APPLYING THE GLAZE

Be sure that the painted piece that you intend to glaze is completely dry and hard. Remove drawers. Place newspapers under the piece for this is a messy job. You will need about a cupful of the ingredients for basic glaze (as given above) for a large piece of furniture, and a brush or a rag to apply the glaze. Use rubber gloves to protect your hands, clean dry rags for wiping the glaze, and a soft dry 1½- or 2-inch brush for brushing the glaze in the final finishing. We use paper towels rather than rags but find that quality varies with brands. Care must be taken to use sturdy varieties that leave no linty residue. Cheesecloth is very satisfactory for wiping the glaze.

The glaze may be applied with a brush or with a rag dipped into the solution. Work on and complete just one section at a time. For large pieces,

17. Children's toys and furniture are ideal for decorating with brightly painted designs.

18. Boxes, bellows, candlesticks and many more ideas for hand-painted gifts and home accessories.

19. Deacon's bench, Early American. The turkey red base color and chrome green trim are enhanced by the peacock design found on page 51.

20. Washstand, Country French. Soft white, lightly antiqued, with floral design and scrolls in green. The trim is pink.

21. Buffet. This is a new piece of furniture painted with a Bavarian motif. Christmas green basic color, ivory panels. The panels are edged with cadmium red and yellow oxide. A heavy umber glaze blends the gaudy colors into a warm, harmonious color scheme.

22. Server. Creamy tan base, dusty rose trim. Swedish designs in blues, pinks and greens. On the front, gourd tree design (page 92). The ends feature a Swedish urn design (page 94).

23. Toy chest. The soft pink is not glazed, for a brighter effect. Page 79 illustrates the rag doll design, filled out here with hearts and flowers.

24. Night stand. It is a rather formal piece, painted in a rather French-Italian style. Antique white and umber glaze. French blue trim with a rose design. Note the heavy spatter here.

25. Peasant chair, a good example of what painting and design can do. This one is painted in the Austrian manner.

26. This desk is a fun thing for tots through teens. The peasant designs are on antique white background, and the trim is blue.

27. This Alpine dining set, painted in a floral and scro[ll] motif, is displayed outside of our shop.

complete each drawer front, side, top or panels separately. Be sure to dab or brush the glaze into corners and depressions. After an area is completely covered, rub the glaze with a soft clean cloth, removing the excess but leaving dark tones in cracks and corners. The center is usually rubbed lighter than the edges.

Now, with the soft *dry* brush, go over the smeary-looking area, brushing in the direction of the grain. If the brush picks up much glaze, wipe it on a cloth to remove excess. As soon as you get the desired effect, stop and do not return again to that section. However, if you are not happy with the results, a little mineral spirits on a rag will remove the glaze and you may try again. The glaze will dry overnight, so if you must remove the glaze, be sure to do it the same day.

Remember, do one section at a time, brush to blend the light and dark areas, and if your first attempt is unsuccessful, remove it and try again. This stage is giving your work a lovely finished look.

SPATTER FINISH

Sometimes an antiqued piece of furniture still has a rather blank look in areas where there are no designs, giving a flat, uninteresting appearance. The spatter finish will help correct that. It also gives a more formal piece of furniture an elegant look.

The spatter finish is applied to an antiqued piece after it has thoroughly dried. To spatter the surface, use the glaze and a dry paintbrush or toothbrush. Try experimenting on an old newspaper in order to get the correct spray, which should be fine, with no big blobs or drips. If possible, avoid holding the brush directly over the piece; rather, stand off and spray at an angle.

Barely dip the brush into the glaze so that just the tip of the brush is wet. Bend the bristles back toward you with a stick so that you can pull the stick over the bristles, allowing them to throw a fine spray of glaze over the furniture. If you get blobs or errors, blot them with a paper towel and try again.

FINAL VARNISH FINISH

If you treat your painted piece with tender loving care, there will be no need for a final coat of varnish. Indeed, after the antiquing glaze has dried well to a hard finish, all that is needed is a coat of wax and a buffing.

However, for table tops, dresser tops, anything that will expect hard wear, we recommend a final coat of varnish.

We have found varnish to be a bit of a problem. Unless you especially want the wet look, even the satin varnishes tend to have too much gloss for folk art. The flat varnish is more appropriate. However, a slight sheen varnish will give the colors more depth. For years we mixed satin and flat varnish in order to get the effect we desired. More recently, we have found Clear Coat (by Martin-Senour Paints) to be a varnish that gives a hand-rubbed look. Clear Coat and satin varnishes can be rubbed lightly with a fine steel wool (when thoroughly dry) for a lower gloss.

For items to be exposed to weather and water, an exterior spar varnish is necessary. We will even go so far as to recommend perpetual care, with a repeat application of spar varnish every year for painted mail-boxes, outdoor signs and garden furniture. Sad but true; you see, we're lazy too! For illustration of step-by-step technique see photos #5 through 11.

CHAPTER NINE

European Folk Designs

A little investigation into the European painted furniture will soon reveal the fact that although each region had its own characteristics, such as color favorites or design elements, there is, nevertheless, many similarities of form and decoration and a basic continuity interwoven throughout Europe.

The rural furniture was pure and decorative, heavily carved or painted or both. In Switzerland, almost everything was painted: beds, cradles, clocks, chests, boxes, and most important, the cupboards. In Denmark, the most common painted pieces were the wardrobes with two doors, most likely painted in a floral motif. All the chairs were either carved or painted and decorated.

In Sweden, folk artists favored designs featuring eagles, dragons, horses, birds and lions. They used much artistic freedom in choosing their colors with little concern for realism (such as red and blue horses). Geometric trees and shrubs abound and, of course, the gourd tree was a favorite and was featured oversized in the street scenes the Swedish loved to paint. The scenes pictured houses with the king's guard and open carriages being pulled by brightly colored horses. The king's guard appeared in full regalia, wearing buttoned waistcoats and tight leggings.

Much of the furniture in Sweden was built into the walls, such as beds and benches. Small chests were often painted with the owner's initials, a date and inscription. Almost every domestic utensil was decorated.

In Norway, *Rosemaling* (meaning rose painting) was an art that was passed down through the families, and it reached its peak in the nineteenth century. Rosemaling is done freehand and features flower and leaf designs with an abundance of scrolls. The Norwegian plume design in very popular and is done with great flourish.

Some of the rural furniture in Italy was made and decorated by peasants and some by professional craftsmen. The furniture done by the shepherds in the mountain areas featured the six-pointed star (used in other countries) or a stag or reindeer. The farmers' painted furniture might include cradles, chairs and dough trays. Flowers were the most popular decoration but religious scenes were also quite popular.

Italian chairs were richly decorated, but by far the most important painted piece in the home of the Italian peasant was the wife's dower chest painted fully with circles, birds and hearts.

The famous Sicilian farm carts were painted with religious scenes or stories from Italian history featuring their national heroes. Every inch of these carts was filled with painted designs.

In Austria, everything is painted, or so it seems! Gates, doors and other architectural details are overflowing with painted designs. "Marriage chairs" were painted fully with dancing figures, clocks, cradles, and headboards were painted with scenes, mostly religious.

German painted furniture is a particular favorite with us. It has a rich robust feeling, featuring reds and blues and many variations of the fruit and flower motif. Scrolls abound to create a fully decorated, rich piece of furniture. South German furniture was made of soft wood and almost always painted. The painted cupboards show the baroque and rococo style as an important influence. The South German or Bavarian furniture featured vases and baskets of flowers (often in a panel), birds, tulips and roses with religious scenes mixed in.

There were painted bride's chairs and small oval boxes called chip boxes, which were decorated with pictures of romantic couples, soldiers, animals, scrolls and flowers. These boxes often had writing on them. It was this heritage that the Pennsylvania Dutch people brought with them to America, continuing in their unique way an art of their own.

On the following pages you will find a selection of European-type designs. Old chests and cupboards with panels are especially adaptable to this sort of design. Panels were often painted with a light ivory background while the rest of the piece might be a rich blue or green. Trim around the panels was often deep gold or red. We find that this type of painted piece looks well when heavily antiqued with a dark glaze.

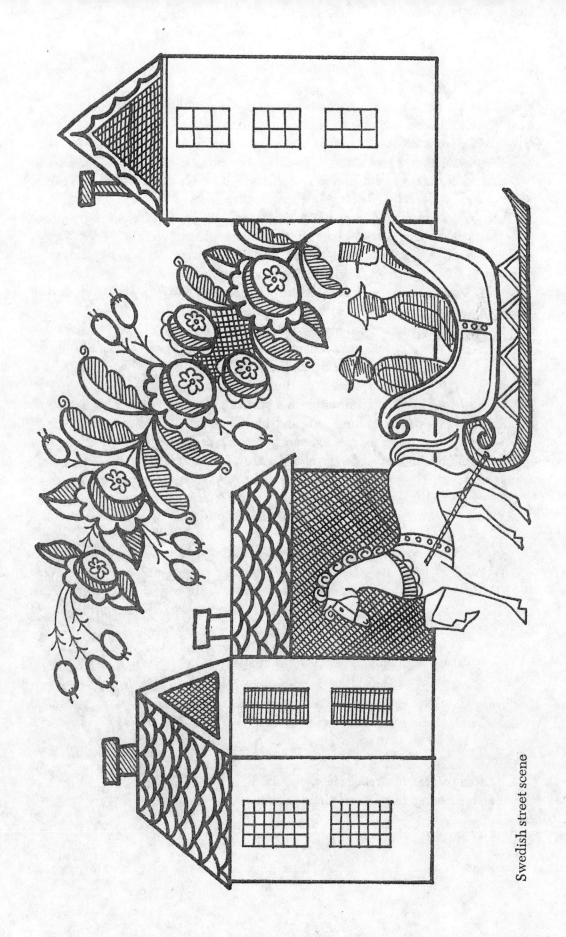

Swedish street scene

The Swedish gourd tree

Often painted in street scenes, oversized
and shooting out from behind houses.

Border design

Swedish peasant art shows a preference for colors of coppery red, soft blues, yellow, leafy greens and dark blue.

93

Borders

Norwegian *Rosemaling* (meaning rose painting).

Use off tones of red, blue and green.
Highlight with yellow and white.

In the Norwegian manner.
A plume design.

97

A design of German origin.
Note the similarity to the Pennsylvania Dutch.

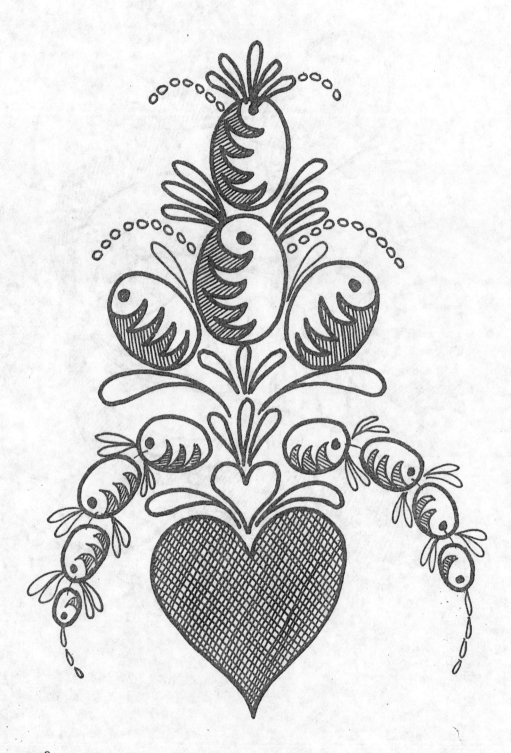

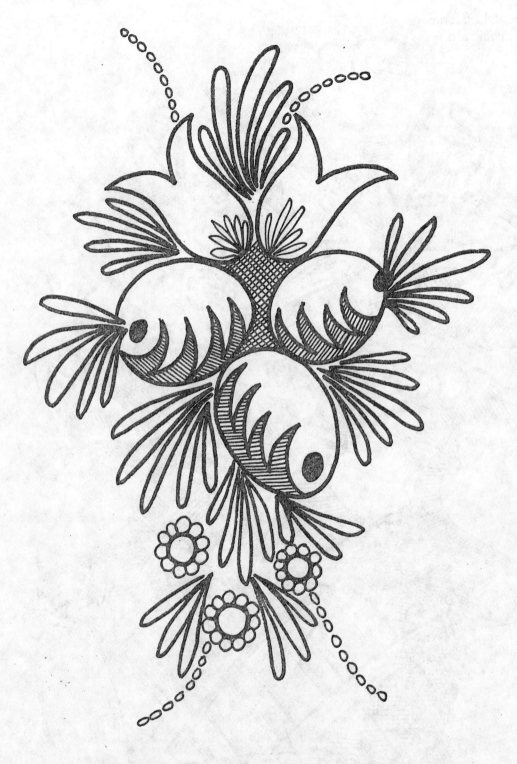

German painted furniture featured florals primarily.

Bavarian style, a form of German folk art.

French ribbon

A French style design, featuring musical instruments and doves.

A favorite theme with the French, and good for an elegant piece of furniture.

Cornucopia. With a French flavor.

This angel could be Italian, German or Austrian; combine it with other designs.

Angels abound in European folk art, carved or painted.

These designs are typical of the Dutch
tile and pottery designs. Most often
painted in shades of blue.

CHAPTER TEN

Decorating with Painted Furniture

Perhaps you have painted a piece of furniture that you are very happy with and wish to decorate your room around it. Make the painted piece the focal point, or center, of interest, using it as your color guide.

If your room is already decorated and you want to paint a piece of furniture to fit into the room, paint the piece a base color that will match or blend. Neutral colors will fit into almost any existing color scheme. These colors are the beige tones, off whites and even the grayed greens. If your wallpaper or fabric has a design, try repeating the design on your painted piece of furniture. Perhaps you wish to be more dramatic. In this case, use the accent color in your room as the base color of your painted piece.

Early American rooms with paneled walls can be sparked up considerably by adding painted furniture and accessories in rich colors such as turkey red, avocado green or mustard. A paneled room can take a goodly amount of painted furniture and accessories with great results.

A monotonous room can be brightened considerably by adding a painted piece of furniture as the focal point. Try a painted desk and a few small painted accessories in a room that is monotonous and uninteresting; these additions can be a relief to the eye.

Do you feel really ambitious? Try painting a complete matching or co-ordinated set of furniture. An uninteresting and drab set of bedroom furniture is perfect for this kind of project. If you haven't a matching set, your challenge may be a room full of unrelated "Early Matrimony" furniture.

All the better! Such a collection of odds and ends can be transformed into a beautifully co-ordinated room. This is a real boon to young marrieds on tight budgets.

If you paint a roomful of furniture as a set, co-ordinate the designs but do not give the decorations equal value. This would prove to be monotonous. Use one piece as your focal point and make the others subordinate to the featured piece. The design for the main painted piece of furniture can be repeated in a less important way on the other pieces. For example, paint a complete design on a large chest or a bed. Then repeat the theme on smaller pieces and accessories by using parts or fragments of the design.

Use your painted piece of furniture as an accent piece with a useful purpose other than adding interest and spice to your home. Consider the following:

- A cumbersome wardrobe can be painted and decorated in light colors and feminine floral designs as extra closet space for the lady of the house.
- A painted chest or cupboard can be used in the hall to store extra linens.
- Paint an armoire for the living room, add shelves inside for the stereo, records, books and games. This could also serve as a concealed bar.
- Washstands can be used in living rooms, kitchens or dining rooms to store china. In a bedroom they are ideal for linens.
- Paint a secretary for the living room or a teen-age girl's bedroom.
- Painted chairs can change the atmosphere of a dining room that is too dark and monotonous with all wood-finished furniture. Consider matching the chair color to the upholstery of the chairs for a decorator touch.

If you have a door with panels, paint them in a color different from the rest of the door. Paint designs in the panels.

If the door is flush and has no architectural interest, cut panels out of plywood and attach. Paint designs.

A bit of the outdoors: Try a mailbox with a touch of whimsey.

For the patio, use a scrub bucket as a wine cooler.

Decorate your window box, wheelbarrow, plant holder.

Flatter your flowers.

And don't forget your birds.

Clay flowerpots are charming
when painted in bright colors
and filled with design.

Or use them to make a pyramid
centerpiece. Glue together three
different size flowerpots. Paint a
little princess and fill her crown
with dried flowers.

At the hardware store, odds and ends.

A tin funnel painted and hanging on the wall makes a string holder.

Paint a tin cup.

A tin pie plate can be hung on the wall for decoration.

Switch plates

Trowels

Flashlights

Paint Fido's house to match yours with a contrasting color for the roof.

Paint in loopy lines for shingles.

A hex sign for good luck.

Be sure to put his name above the door.

Paint a garden of daisies.

Be sure to finish with a coat of spar varnish.

Paint stair risers. Use several colors, then add designs.

Ways to create a cooky jar.

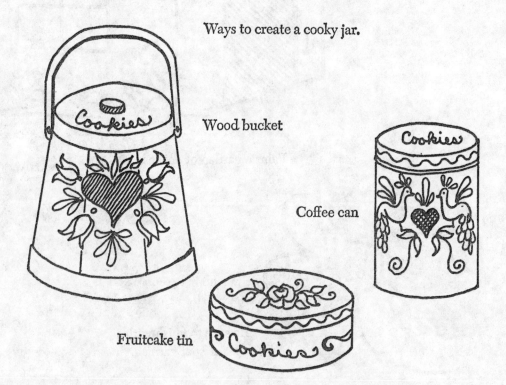

Wood bucket

Coffee can

Fruitcake tin

116

Paint on glass. Paint directly on clear glass with the special enamels used for glass painting (at the art supply shop).

Pitcher and glass set

Or paint a glass bottle the way you would paint furniture: base coat, antique glaze. This gives the effect of pottery.

Old jelly jars used as a spice set.

Make a toothbrush set. Match a brush and plastic or glass drinking cup.

117

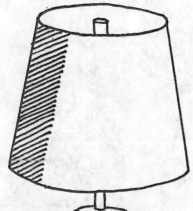

Lamps. Make your lamps from your painted accessories.

Have your lamp wired at a lamp shop, or a handyman can do it.

Cut and glue felt to the base (underneath) to avoid scratches on your table.

Weight your base by filling with sand or plaster of Paris.

Use your imagination in choosing lamp base.

118

To make a mirror more important, cut a piece of plywood in the size you want and attach your mirror. Paint it as a unit and add designs. Match it to a piece of painted furniture for a custom look.

Co-ordinate your window shade and cornice. Consider repeating a design from your curtains on the cornice board.

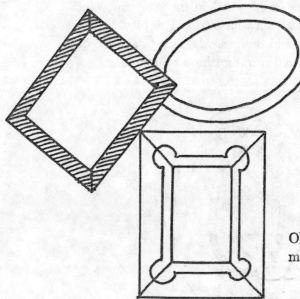

Old discarded picture frames
make delightful trays.

Remove glass and attach plywood backing.
Paint and apply designs. Seal with varnish.
Great for gifts.

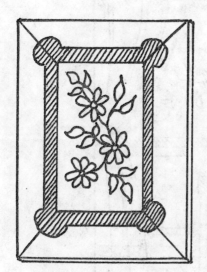  

Make a plant stand out of an old bed-post and a salad bowl. Nail a round wood base at bottom, paint gaily.

Cannister set. Paint your old set or old assorted cans.

Paint a shelf to match.

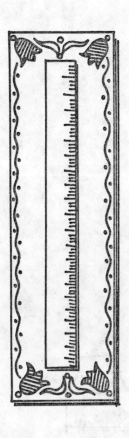

Make a "grow up stick."

Glue or tack a wood yardstick to a piece of plywood that you have painted in a bright color. Paint designs and the child's name.

Paint a tray, jars and a box to match for a nursery.

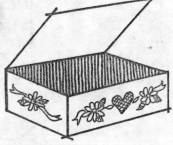

Use our designs for appliquéd pillows. Cut a different color piece for each unit of the design and sew on plain "store bought" pillows.

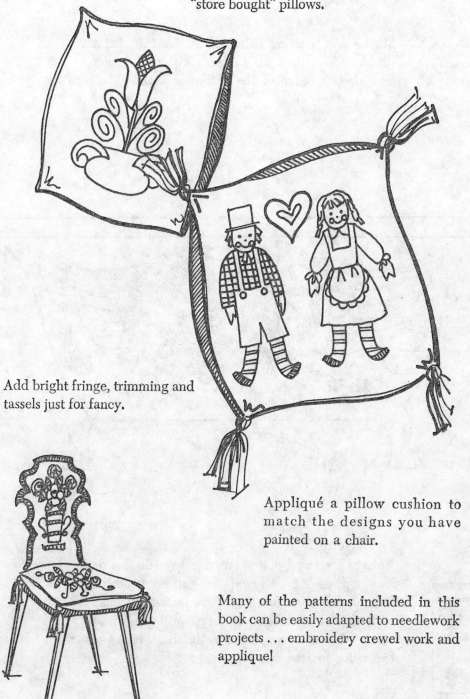

Add bright fringe, trimming and tassels just for fancy.

Appliqué a pillow cushion to match the designs you have painted on a chair.

Many of the patterns included in this book can be easily adapted to needlework projects . . . embroidery crewel work and applique!

Maybe you have an old bathtub like this. Paint the outside with a bright shocking accent color or a deeper shade of the bathroom walls.

Enlarge the angel design on page 105 (do this on a large piece of brown wrapping paper). Paint the face of the angel first and then just keep going with the wings, adding feathers until the whole side of the tub is covered. Use different shades of one color for the wings.

Cut a headboard out of plywood. Add square posts on sides and glue a drapery rod finial to the top of the post.

A guardhouse and soldier for boys.

Mod flowers for a teen-age girl.

How about Pennsylvania Dutch for a guest room?

For a Bavarian style, nail a small picture frame to the headboard for a panel. Paint panel ivory, bed a rich color. Add border on side posts, designs on panel and scrolls to finish. Presto!

Paint a seven-day chest with the days of the week on each drawer, maybe in French.

Or a chest for a child's room with a drawer for shirts, socks, pants, etc. Paint it in your own handwriting.

Surprise! Paint only the inside lid of a cedar chest with gay designs, a name and date.

Make a cushion for the cedar chest. Sew on huge yarn tassels and you have a bench.

Try a continuous design to cover entirely the front of a chest. Let the design flow over drawers and dividers.

Also, paint your design on the wall behind the bed.

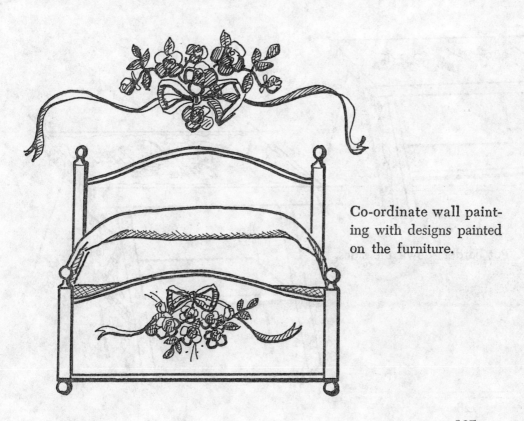

Co-ordinate wall painting with designs painted on the furniture.

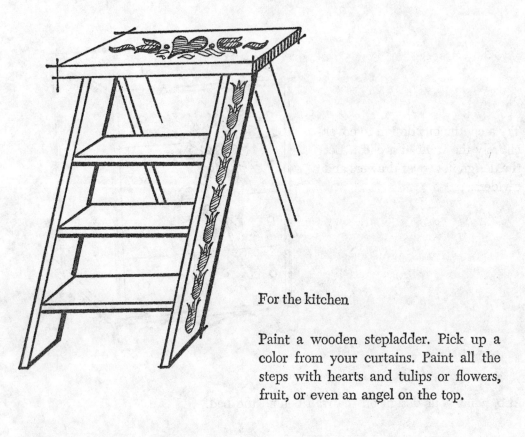

For the kitchen

Paint a wooden stepladder. Pick up a color from your curtains. Paint all the steps with hearts and tulips or flowers, fruit, or even an angel on the top.

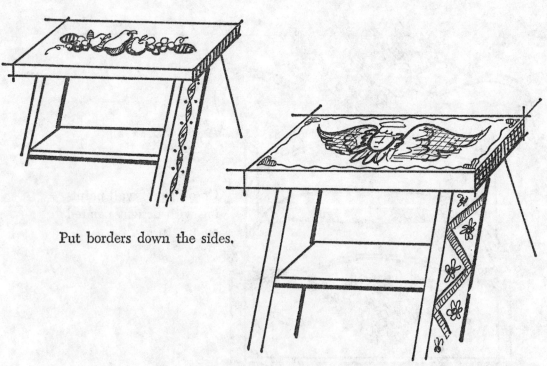

Put borders down the sides.

FINIS

And so dear reader, we leave you with your new adventure, creating lovely and fun things. May all your projects be happy ones. Good luck and best wishes.

Joyce and Jeanne

FOR FURTHER READING

Christiansen, E. O., *Index of American Design*. New York, The Macmillan Company.

Grotz, George, *Furniture Doctor*. New York, Doubleday and Company, Inc.

Hansen, H. J., ed., *European Folk Art*. New York, McGraw-Hill Book Company.

Lichten, Frances, *Folk Art of Rural Pennsylvania*. New York, Charles Scribner's Sons.

Margon, Lester, *Masterpieces of European Furniture*. New York, Architectural Book Publishing Co., Inc.

Robacker, Earl F., *Touch of the Dutchland*. New York, A. S. Barnes and Co., Inc.